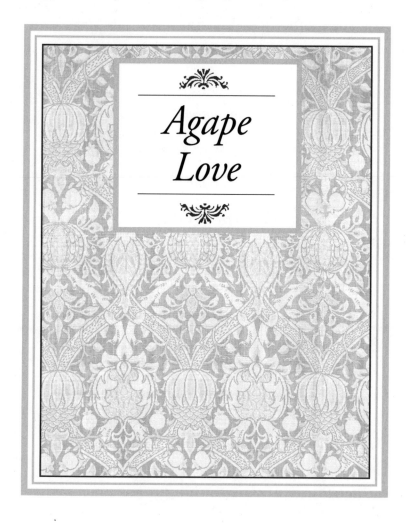

Agape
Love

Lord, make me an instrument of your peace.

Where there is hatred, let me sow love;

Where there is injury, pardon;

Where there is doubt, faith;

Where there is despair, hope;

Where there is darkness, light;

Where there is sadness, joy.

—St. Francis of Assisi

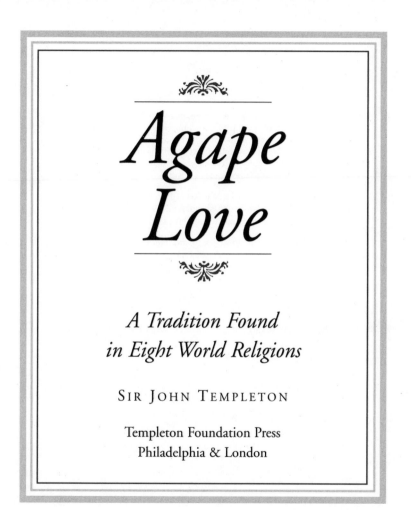

Agape Love

A Tradition Found in Eight World Religions

SIR JOHN TEMPLETON

Templeton Foundation Press
Philadelphia & London

Templeton Foundation Press
Five Radnor Corporate Center, Suite 120
Radnor, Pennsylvania 19087

Biblical quotations are from the New Revised Standard Version of the
Bible, © 1989 by the Division of Christian Education of the National
Council of the Churches of Christ in the USA.

Library of Congress Cataloging-in-Publication Data

Templeton, John, 1912–
    Agape love : a tradition found in eight world religions / John
Templeton.
        p.   cm.
    ISBN 1-890151-29-7 (alk. paper)
    1. Love—Religious aspects Comparative studies.   I. Title.
BL626.4.T45   1999
291.5'677—dc21   99–37801
                                                        CIP

Special thanks to research associates Randall Frame and Michelle Gorman
Text and jacket design by Joanna Hill and Helene Krasney
Typeset in Adobe Garamond
Printed and bound by Data Reproductions

"Granada" pattern used on dust jacket is by William Morris;
courtesy of the Trustees of the Victoria and Albert Museum, London.

99 00 01 02 03 04 05 06   10 9 8 7 6 5 4 3 2 1

Contents

Introduction

Agape love means feeling and expressing pure, unlimited love for every human being with no exception. Developing such divine ability has been a goal for me for almost all of my eighty-six years on earth.

This does not mean you need to admire each person or to weaken legal penalties for crimes. It does mean that if your mother were murdered, you should try to eliminate the poisons of hatred or revenge. While a murderer is being properly punished and prevented from a criminal life, agape love allows you to pray for his conversion and his soul.

Numerous researchers have helped me explore concepts of unlimited love in eight major religions. I am only a student and beginner in the research and practice of this fruitful and basic reality called "agape love." I hope that each reader of this little book will contribute his or her own fruitful thoughts on the nature and enormous benefits of agape love.

The rich variety of world religions creates a tapestry of amazing beauty—a testimony to the essential spiritual nature of our human existence. And yet, within this amazing and sometimes fascinating diversity can be found an equally amazing unity, the basis of which is "love." Perhaps without even being fully aware of it, religious leaders and their followers through the ages have defined religion largely in terms of love. All the world's great religions, to varying degrees, both teach and assume the priority of love in religious practice. To put it another way, whether consciously or subconsciously, the world seems to have determined that any system of beliefs that teaches or tolerates hatred or even apathy toward others does not deserve to be considered a religion in the first place.

As the Dalai Lama has stated, "All the major religions of the world have similar ideals of love, the same goal of benefiting humanity through spiritual practice, and the same effect of making their followers into better human beings."

Within Western culture, love has been defined in countless ways. To the philosopher, it is the "eternal emotion"; to the songwriter, "a many-splendored thing." The fact that it takes so many definitions to capture the meaning of love suggests that its meaning cannot be fully captured after all, at least within the limitations of language. It is more accurately measured in action—in good will, kindness, forgiveness, and compassion toward others.

For our single word "love," the ancient Greeks used several words in an effort to clarify love's various shades of meaning. They distinguished, for example, between the romantic love shared by husband and wife, and the "brotherly love" that exists among friends.

But the highest kind of love gained expression for the ancient Greeks in the term *agape.* Agape love is not directed toward a single person or small group of friends, but toward all humanity, even all of creation. Agape love is not based on how we are treated by others. Rather, it is unconditional and unlimited in its expression. It is this kind of love in which the religions of the world may find a basis for unity.

Agape love comes closest to describing the kind of love with which the Creator loves the creation. Agape love is pure love, unlimited in its possibilities. Agape love is altruistic love, love that is given for its own sake, without expecting anything in return.

Religion provides both the structure and the principles to guide this universal spiritual need. To those who are looking, it is not hard to find fundamental principles shared by the world's religious traditions in their efforts to move adherents toward the goal of loving as God loves.

One such principle is known within Christianity as the Golden Rule: "Do unto others as you would have them do unto you." A Buddhist would say, "Hurt not others with that which pains yourself." A follower of Confucius would say: "What you yourself do not desire, do not put before others." Islam states it as follows: "Do unto all men as you would wish to have done unto you." And Hinduism says: "This is the sum of true righteousness—treat others as you would yourself be treated."

Other principles shared by the world's great religions include the goal of alleviating human suffering, avoiding harm to others, and the striving toward empathy; that is, learning to identify with the needs of others, especially those who are most vulnerable to the world's ills. These interrelated principles are all firmly rooted in the commitment to pursue agape love.

The purpose of this book is not to conclude that all religions are the same, for certainly they are not. Nor is its goal to try to convert anyone from one religion to another. Rather, the purpose is to point toward the possibilities and responsibilities of love. It is to awaken people to the realization that despite the differences, all religions share some very important, fundamental principles and goals, the highest of which is the realization of agape love—unconditional, unlimited, pure love.

The Native American poet Manitongquat wrote:

> Life is the Sacred Mystery singing to itself,
> dancing to its drum, telling tales, improvising, playing
> and we are all that Spirit,
> our stories all but one cosmic story
> that we are love indeed,
> that perfect love in me seeks the love in you,
> and if our eyes could ever meet without fear
> we would recognize each other and rejoice,
> for love is life believing in itself.

All the world's people, whatever their religious beliefs, are part of the same family. We all have the same general needs, problems, desires, and dreams. When we embrace the possibility of agape love, we are expressing, amidst our differences, a unity of purpose, a common hope. At the dawn of the third millennium, what vision could be more important?

O Love, O pure deep love,

be here, be now.

Be all; worlds dissolve

into your stainless endless radiance,

Frail living leaves burn with you

brighter than cold stars:

Make me your servant,

your breath, your core.

—RUMI,

PERSIAN SUFI POET

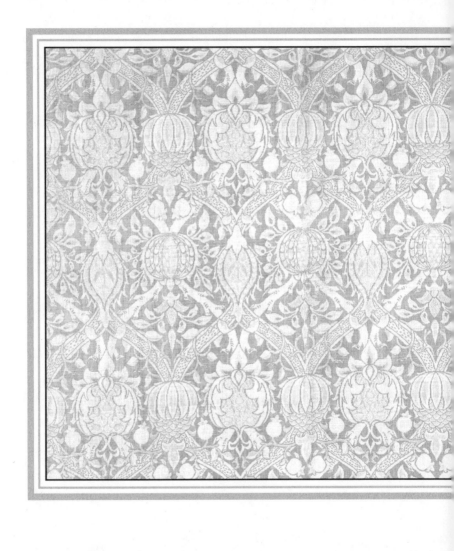

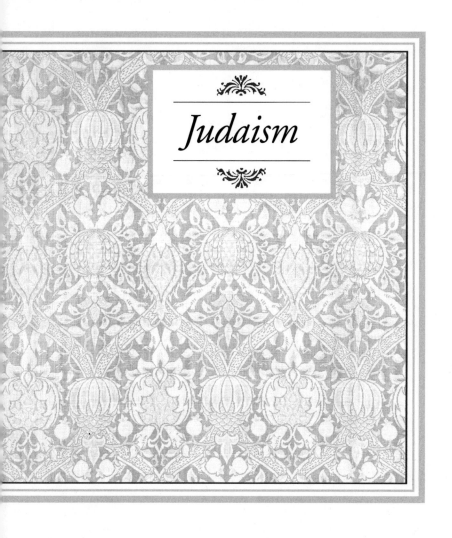

Judaism

What does the Lord require of you

but to do justice, and to love kindness,

and to walk humbly with your God?

—MICAH 6:8

Salvation is attained not by subscription

to metaphysical dogmas, but solely by the love of God

that fulfills itself in action.

This is the cardinal truth of Judaism.

—CHASDAI CRESCAS, 1410

Judaism

Agape lies at the very foundations of the Jewish faith. The book of Genesis affirms that God pronounced all of creation "good." It states that all human beings have been created in the image and likeness of God. Agape seems the only appropriate response to those who bear God's image.

Deuteronomy 6:5 states that "You shall love the Lord your God with all your heart, and with all your soul, and with all your might." This reminds followers that love toward God is essential, and that one way it is expressed is by using one's powers of goodness to benefit others. In fact, when one loves and cares for others, one is loving God.

Early in Genesis, Cain learns a lesson intended for all— that we are our "brother's keeper," even when it seems incon-

To do righteousness and justice

is more acceptable to the Lord than sacrifice.

—Proverbs 21:3

David, you're a better person than I am. You treated me with kindness, even though I've been cruel to you. You've told me how you were kind enough not to kill me when the Lord gave you the chance. If you really were my enemy, you wouldn't have let me leave here alive. I pray that the Lord will give you a big reward for what you did today.

—Based on 1 Samuel 24:16-19

venient. That is, human beings are responsible for the welfare of others.

The command to love one's neighbor, found in the book of Leviticus, is central to the Jewish faith. Several Hebrew words were used in the Torah to express the concept of agape. Taken together, these words understand agape in terms of such related concepts as goodness, lovingkindness, and mercy.

From the Hebrew Bible we are given one of the most beautiful images of agape in the form of one of recorded history's deepest friendships, the one between Jonathan and David. The author of 1 Samuel writes that "the soul of Jonathan was bound to the soul of David, and Jonathan loved him as his own soul"(18:1). Jonathan's loyalties were divided between his friend and his father, King Saul, who was obsessed with jealousy toward David. Jonathan chose his friend. Later on, David returned the kindness by not killing Saul when he had the opportunity.

Agape is also expressed in terms of God's boundless concern for the poor and the hungry. In fact, the Passover festival

Let justice roll down like waters,

and righteousness like an everflowing stream.

—AMOS 5:24

If I am not for myself, who will be for me?

And if I am only for myself, what am I?

And if not now, when?

—HILLEL, TALMUDIC SCHOLAR AND SAGE

retells the story of Moses leading his people out of Egypt to the promised land. At the Passover Seder dinner, in addition to the use of symbolic foods, rituals, songs, and prayers, special attention is paid to spiritual and political freedom. Prayers are said for all of those who do not enjoy the freedom given by God, who shows mercy, compassion, and justice to all. Participants are reminded that some are not yet redeemed until all are free. So as thanks are given for our present blessings, there is a deep sense of responsibility to help all others who are not as fortunate.

Among the greatest legacies of Judaism has been its focus on fulfilling responsibilities and duties. Agape is not just warm feelings; it is also action. It entails being true to the commitment made to God, to the Ten Commandments, and to the responsibilities toward family and neighbor as set forth in these eternal precepts.

The world would do well to come to a greater appreciation of agape as fulfilling our responsibilities and commitments. There is something positive to be said for getting in touch

Whatever is hateful unto thee, do it not

unto thy fellow. This is the whole Law.

The rest is commentary.

—HILLEL

You shall not take vengeance or bear a grudge

against any of your people, but you shall love

your neighbor as yourself.

—LEVITICUS 19:17

with our feelings. But sometimes responsibilities and obligations must be carried out in spite of feelings.

Feelings may be fleeting, but the obligations of agape do not change. A father loves his children when he spends time with them even when he doesn't always feel like it. Someone who feels romantically attracted to a person other than his or her spouse is nevertheless morally obligated to remain faithful. When other people are in need, we are commanded to come to their aid, even though for one reason or another we may not want to. In the Jewish faith, this act of kindness for its own sake is called a mitzvah. One of the most central is the mitzvah of Tzedakah, which means charity, but also the moral obligation to help others in need.

Agape is central to the core of Judaism. Love of God means loving oneself and others. It means turning to goodness, truth, mercy, and charity to direct our actions. For the Jew, love of God means living an ethical life according to the highest order of tradition, sharing the bounty, teaching the Jewish heritage to children, controlling harsh or hurtful words, and making

Give justice to the weak and the orphan;

Maintain the right of the lowly and the destitute.

Rescue the weak and the needy;

Deliver them from the hand of the wicked.

—Psalm 82:3–4

life sacred. A Jew who seeks to fulfill each Commandment with love is on the path of holiness. Agape lives within us all. It is found in that "still small voice."

The Still Small Voice

Listen to the still small voice.
It tells us to follow
   in the ways of holiness.
It asks us to sanctify our days
   with kindness.
The still small voice is not in the wind,
   the shaking of the earth, or in fire.
The still small voice
   is heard in the hearts
   of those who listen.

—Esta Cassway
Based on 1 Kings 19:11–12

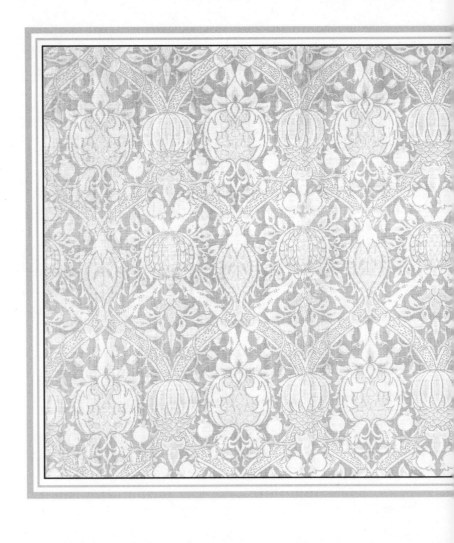

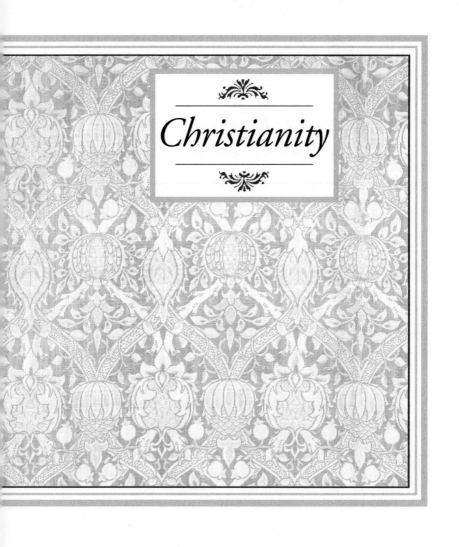

Christianity

Love is patient; love is kind; love is not envious or

boastful or arrogant or rude. It does not insist on its

own way; it is not irritable or resentful;

it does not rejoice in wrongdoing, but rejoices in the

truth. It bears all things, believes all things,

hopes all things, endures all things.

—1 CORINTHIANS 13:4–7

Christianity

The Bible proclaims that God is love. The main messages and themes of Scripture revolve around God's unconditional love for all creation. Many people cannot escape images of God as a demanding and vengeful judge eager to punish all who fail to live as they should. But through his actions and through his teachings, Jesus Christ portrayed a different kind of God.

As described in the gospel of Mark, when a scribe came forward to ask Jesus what was the most important commandment of all, Jesus replied, "You shall love the Lord your God with all your heart, soul, mind, and strength." Then Jesus added, "The second is this, 'You shall love your neighbor as yourself'" (Mark 12:28–34).

When self-righteous religious leaders of Jesus' day sought to

And now faith, hope, and love abide, these three;

and the greatest of these is love.

—1 CORINTHIANS 13:13

Above all, maintain constant love for one another,

for love covers a multitude of sins.

—1 PETER 4:8

Therefore be imitators of God, as beloved children,

and live in love, as Christ loved us.

—EPHESIANS 5:1-2

stone to death a woman caught in the act of adultery, they no doubt thought they were acting as representatives of God. But Jesus interceded in the woman's behalf and pointed to a different way. "Whoever among you is without sin," he said, "let him cast the first stone" (John 8:2–11).

The Bible portrays a God who loves *all* people: the rich and the poor, the weak and the powerful. God's love is unconditional. Nothing, not even behavior that falls short of the standards established by Scripture, can prevent God from loving all his children.

One of the most moving examples Jesus used to reveal the loving character of God focuses on a shepherd with one hundred sheep under his care. One of those sheep has gone astray and is lost. To a modern-day, pragmatic businessman, ninety-nine out of one hundred would likely sound pretty good. Maybe even eighty out of one hundred would be acceptable as long as he can "write off" the other twenty on his tax return. But God is not a pragmatist. God is described as an idealist who is not satisfied with ninety-

What anyone does out of love

remains inscribed on his heart,

for love is the fire of life, and so constitutes

the life in everyone. Consequently, as the love is,

so the life is; and as the life is,

that is as the love is, so the entire person is

in soul and in body.

—EMANUEL SWEDENBORG

seven or ninety-eight or even ninety-nine sheep safely in the fold.

Images come to mind of a cold, dark, rainy night and of a loving shepherd braving the elements, searching desperately, never quitting until the lost sheep is found again. The God of Christianity, like the brave shepherd, will keep searching high and low for those who have gone astray. God's love will not be limited. It will never tire no matter how dark or cold the night.

Such is a model for Christians to give. The gospel writer John records Jesus as saying, "This is my commandment, that you love one another as I have loved you. Greater love has no man than this, that a man lay down his life for his friends."

But agape in the Christian context also means loving enemies. In his Sermon on the Mount, Jesus preached, "You have heard that it was said, 'You shall love your neighbor and hate your enemy.' But I say to you, Love your enemies and pray for those who persecute you."

Jesus began the Sermon on the Mount with the Beatitudes, which set forth the kinds of attitudes consistent with agape:

Those who say, "I love God,"

and hate their brothers or sisters, are liars.

—1 John 4:20

Beloved, let us love one another,

because love is from God;

everyone who loves is born of God

and knows God.

—1 John 4:7

Blessed are the poor in spirit, the meek, the merciful, the pure in heart, the peacemakers.

Perhaps none of Jesus' words illustrate his admonition to agape better than the parable of the Good Samaritan. He has just told his listeners to love their neighbors and someone has asked, "Who is my neighbor?" (Some of his listeners no doubt interpreted "neighbor" to mean "fellow Israelite.")

Now in Jesus' time, Jews and Samaritans despised one another. In two thousand years it seems little has changed, as ethnic groups in the Middle East, Eastern Europe, the Balkans, and elsewhere live in constant tension. According to the parable, a Jewish man is attacked on his way to Jericho. Two representatives of the religious establishment ignored him before a Samaritan finally came to his aid. Not only did the Samaritan rescue the man, but he transported him to an inn and in essence said to the innkeeper, "Send me the bill." The lesson for Jesus' listeners and for us today is that with agape, all people are neighbors and the responsibilities of love know no limits.

Only as we learn to love God and others do

we gain real freedom and autonomy in a society

in which most people live in a state of slavery

to their own needs and desires.

—ROBERTA BONDI

Jesus told his disciples that they can show their love for God by looking after those in need. In the book of Matthew, he speaks of a God who is mysteriously present among those who are weak and vulnerable: the hungry, the naked, the outcast, the sick, the imprisoned. Jesus taught that those who feed the hungry, clothe the naked, welcome the outcast, care for the sick, and visit the prisoner are in a very real way serving and loving God.

Jesus further illustrates the priority of agape by healing on the Sabbath. When he did so, lawyers and Pharisees accused him of violating religious law. But Jesus responded in essence that agape trumps religious custom. No time is a wrong time to heal, to love.

Christian love is not an isolated action. Rather, it is a way of life, a habit in search of constant expression. No time for agape is too soon. No setting for agape is inappropriate, no recipient of agape unworthy. Such is the nature of boundless, unconditional love. ❧

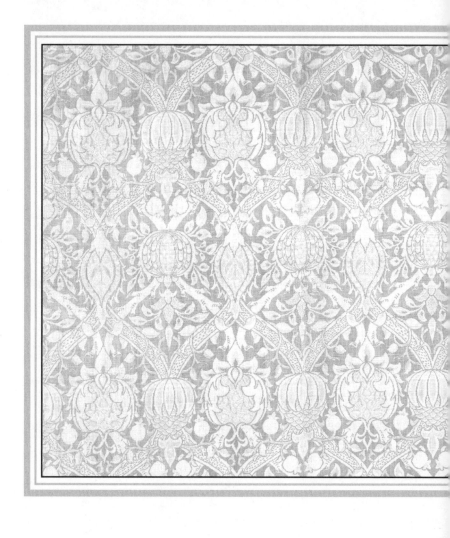

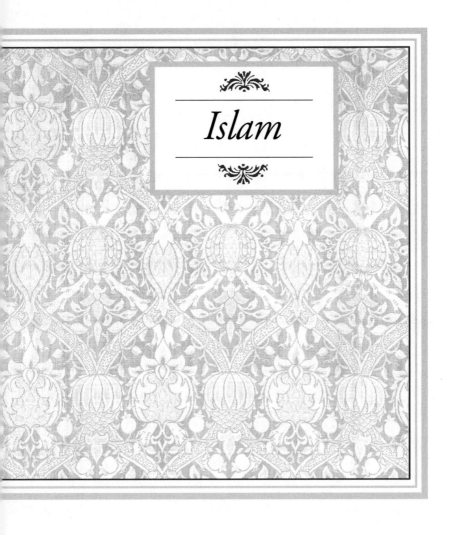

Islam

[Paradise will be occupied by] those

who love one another for God's sake,

those who sit together for God's sake,

and those who visit one another for God's sake.

—FROM THE HADITH

Islam

One does not have to look far to discover the call to agape in the Islamic context. The opening chapter of the Qur'an, in two of the first three lines, refers to Allah as "the Merciful, the Compassionate." Indeed, mercy and compassion are primary attributes of God, and followers of God are called upon to embrace these characteristics.

The Qur'an contains over 190 references to God's mercy and compassion. Ameer Ali, in *The Spirit of Islam,* speaks of Allah as

> the Holy, the Peaceful, the Faithful, the Guardian over His servants, the Shelterer of the orphan, the Guide of the erring, the Deliverer from every affliction, the Friend

Do you give something that you value greatly, something that you love? If you give your life in a cause, that is the greatest gift you can give. If you give yourself, that is, your personal efforts, your talents, your skill, your learning, that comes next in degree. If you give your earnings, your property, your possessions, that is also a great gift; for many people love them even more than other things. And there are less tangible things, such as positions, reputation, the well-being of those we love, the regard of those who can help us, etc. It is unselfishness that God demands, and there is no act of unselfishness, however small or tangible, but is well within the knowledge of God.

—FROM THE QUR'AN, FOOTNOTE 419

(TRANS. A. YUSUF ALI)

36

of the bereaved, the Consoler of the afflicted; in His hand is good, and He is the generous Lord, the Gracious, the Hearer, the Near-at-Hand, the Compassionate, the Merciful, the Very-forgiving, whose love for man is more tender than that of the mother-bird for her young.

Islam teaches that love for God is corroborated through love for neighbors, and in fact all beings, and that it is impossible for those who do evil to love God.

One of the five pillars of the Islamic faith is the obligation to charity, that is, the admonition to come to the aid of the less fortunate. The Qur'an instructs those who would follow God not only to do for others what they would have others do for them, but to "give in full what is due from you, whether you expect or wish to receive full consideration from the other side or not." (Qur'an, footnote 6011, as translated by A. Yusuf Ali) In fact, the Qur'an calls for an annual distribution to the needy of one-fortieth, not only of monetary income for the year, but a number of one's possessions specified by Islamic Law.

A man served God for seventy years and then

committed a sin which canceled the merit

of his service. Afterwards he gave a loaf of bread

to a poor man, so God pardoned his sin and gave

him back the merit of his seventy years' service.

His alms are vain who does not know that his need

of the reward for giving is greater than

the poor man's need of the gift.

—MUSLIM SAYING

Suras 2:177 and 4:36 call upon followers to give their material possessions to their families, to orphans and travelers, even to beggars and strangers. Sura 51:19 contains especially profound insights into the nature of agape. "True charity," it reads, "remembers not only those in need who ask, but also those who are prevented by some reason from asking." The truly charitable person seeks out those in need who do not or cannot ask for help.

The passage goes on to suggest reasons people in need do not ask for help: perhaps they are ashamed, perhaps they are unaware of their need or of others' capacity to help. Or a person may not be able to voice his need. As the Qur'an puts it, "He may be a dumb and helpless creature, whether a human being or a dumb animal or any creature within your ken of power."

Agape in this passage means reaching out for others instead of waiting until they come to us, for they may never be able to do so. It means seeking out those in need as we would search desperately for a lost pet or a valuable family heirloom. And it

The descendents of Adam are members of one body,

For from the moment of Creation they are made

of a single substance.

If the hands of fate causes pain in a single member,

The other members will lose their

tranquility and peace.

If thou are not saddened by the affliction of others,

Thou art not worthy to be called human.

SA'DĪ, THIRTEENTH-CENTURY

PERSIAN POET

(TRANS. S.H.NASR)

is not enough to meet the material need. We must meet the need in ways that affirm human dignity and pride, that minister to another person's spirit and emotions with special sensitivity and wisdom.

Perfunctory welfare programs, no matter how supposedly efficient, may be useful and necessary, but they do not represent agape according to Islam. Rather, we are enjoined to love proactively, to go out and find those who are in need of mercy and compassion, and to meet their needs with special sensitivity, wisdom, and caring. We are called to be a voice for the voiceless, to be sensitive to unexpressed need, to respond to those whose cries for help cannot be heard. In doing so, we become ambassadors of agape.

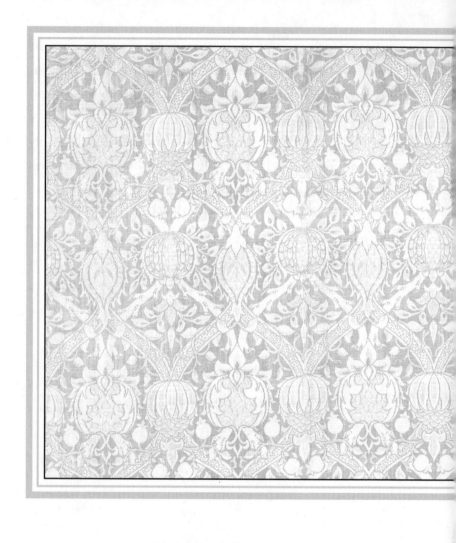

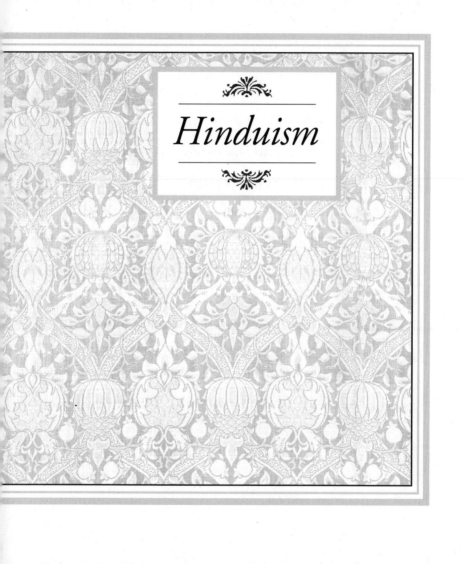

Hinduism

Such power as I possess

in the political field has derived

from my experiments in the spiritual field.

—GANDHI IN HIS AUTOBIOGRAPHY

Hinduism

The introduction to this book points out that most of the world's great religious traditions contain some version of the Golden Rule, which urges followers to treat others as they want to be treated themselves. Some scholars have observed that according to the Hindu Laws of Manu, the ten duties all must carry out—regardless of class or stage of life—can be summarized by the Golden Rule.

The Hindu religion provides the ultimate rationale for the ethic prescribed by the Golden Rule, for it teaches that all reality is ultimately one in being and in function.

Hinduism speaks of the self, or soul *(Atman)*. It also speaks of *Brahman* as being the ultimate principle of the universe. The fundamental religious conviction that Brahman is Atman,

I met a hundred men on the road to Delhi,

and they all were my brothers.

—INDIAN PROVERB

If given with love, a handful is sufficient.

—TELUGU PROVERB

or that the self is ultimately inseparable from the whole, lays a firm foundation for agape in the Hindu context.

Because all human beings are in some sense one, and indeed because all of creation is one, the only way to treat others is with respect, kindness, justice, and compassion. An excerpt from the *Brihad-Aranyaka Upanishad* illustrates this principle:

> Not for love of the husband is a husband dear,
> but for love of the Soul *(Atman)* a husband is dear.
> Not for love of the wife is a wife dear,
> but for love of the Soul a wife is dear.
> Not for love of all is all dear,
> but for the love of the Soul is all dear.

Hinduism has contributed to the world an emphasis on inner consciousness, illumination, attaining to higher levels of spirituality. Hindu spirituality recognizes that there is meaning beyond the individual self and beyond material possessions and earthly pleasures. This emphasis does not come at the expense of agape, but rather as a supplement to it. As

Love is all important and its own reward.

—TAMIL PROVERB

Lord, I do not want wealth,

nor children, nor learning. If it be Thy will

I will go to a hundred hells, but grant me this,

that I may love Thee without the hope of reward,

unselfishly love for love's sake.

—HINDU PRAYER

Huston Smith puts it, "Religion is always more than morality, but if it lacks a moral base, it will not stand." Indeed, most branches of Hinduism teach high moral principles. The moral law contained within the *Mahabharata* emphasizes kindness to all creatures. Thus, agape can be viewed as a natural course of action for those operating at a high level of spirituality.

The Hindu holy text, the *Bhagavad-Gita,* teaches that those seeking ultimate spiritual freedom are characterized by such qualities as compassion and generosity. Liberation requires fleeing immorality. Smith observes that through Hinduism, "myriads have transformed the will-to-get into the will-to-give, the will-to-win into the will-to-serve." This holy book, although a treatise on war, encourages striving for a higher level of spirituality with such qualities as compassion, generosity, and nonviolence.

Perhaps no person has exemplified the relationship between deep spirituality and agape more than Mohandas Gandhi. After becoming a victim of racial prejudice while living in South Africa, he was not content merely to defend himself.

"Why do you keep rescuing that scorpion

when its only gratitude is to bite you?"

The yogi replied, "It is the nature

of scorpions to bite. It is the nature of yogis

to help others when they can."

—TRADITIONAL STORY

Rather, he set out to change the world for all people. He turned to a life of prayer, fasting, and asceticism as he developed his political and social philosophy, which eventually found expression in the practice of *satyagraha.*

Satyagraha called for civil disobedience in order to protest unjust laws, laws that caused human suffering and assaulted human dignity. Participants must be prepared to face the physical and legal consequences of their actions, for their civil disobedience was to be practiced nonviolently, with an attitude of love.

Satyagraha included an element of *bhakti* yoga, which is the way of loving devotion to God. Gandhi called upon his followers to view their actions as an offering of their bodies and souls to God.

The most profound feature of satyagraha is the one that most reveals the presence of agape. Gandhi taught that the ultimate goal was not to remove the burden from the oppressed, but to change the very hearts and minds of the oppressor. This represents unlimited, unconditional love and

The world is a theatre of love.

—KASHMIRI PROVERB

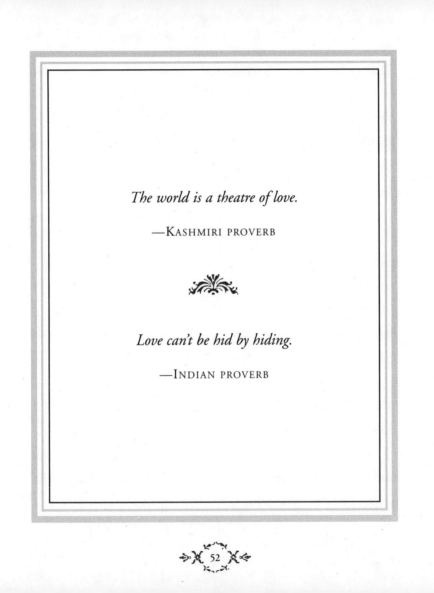

Love can't be hid by hiding.

—INDIAN PROVERB

reflects the Hindu philosophy that all people, even our enemies, are a part of the same ultimate reality.

Gandhi's peaceful, agapelike leadership led India to political freedom. When Gandhi died early in 1948 from an assassin's bullet, this man of less than one hundred pounds had a mere two dollars to his name.

The utility of satyagraha makes sense in light of the sociological research that many victimizers in society—those who steal or kill, who abuse emotionally or physically—were once themselves victims of physical or emotional abuse or neglect. Agape is too generous to leave such persons behind. It calls for an end to the cycle of violence. It points toward a different way.

In the Hindu context, agape is a byproduct of bhakti yoga, the realization of God through love. To the bhakti yogi, compassionate love is the highest vehicle to union with God. As one works on purifying motives and being of service, a higher state of consciousness results, and agape follows as a natural expression of this state. In pursuing God, one

Love alone will abide thee.

—TAMIL PROVERB

becomes more like God, and agape follows as a natural consequence.

We can learn from Hinduism that spirituality is a two-way path. The desire to look inward inevitably produces an outward manifestation of selfless love for all creation—agape.

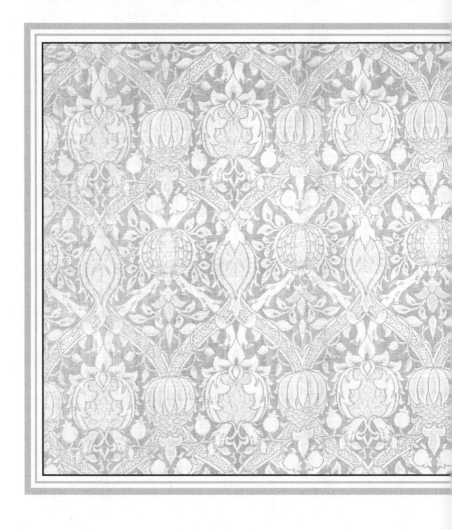

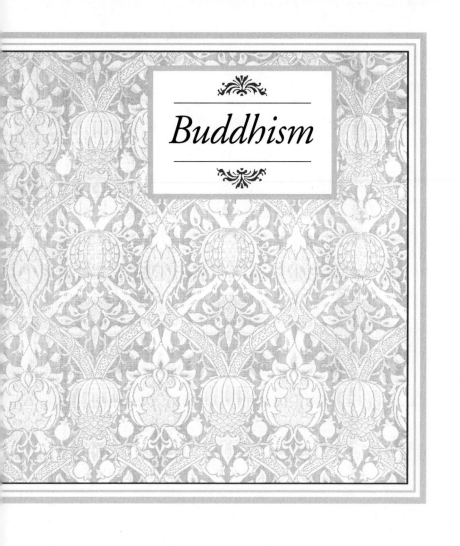

Buddhism

However innumerable beings are,

I vow to save them.

—ONE OF THE FOUR VOWS OF THE BODHISATTVA

In Buddhism, the source of moral authority

is the causal law. Be kind, be just, be humane,

be honest if you desire to crown your future.

Dishonesty, cruelty, inhumanity will

condemn you to a miserable fall.

—SOYEN SHAKU

Buddhism

In a sense, the religion of Buddhism itself was born out of agape, out of a willingness to sacrifice on behalf of the suffering people of the world. The history of Buddhism can be traced to the life of Siddhartha Gautama (563-483 B.C.E.). He was born a prince and reared in luxury. He lived in a palace with a beautiful wife and son. He had all the material wealth for which any reasonable person could ask. But none of that could fulfill his desire to live a life full of meaning and purpose.

Legend has it that one day upon venturing forth from his palace Gautama encountered a beleaguered, trembling old man. On another day he witnessed someone lying by the roadside, overcome by disease. On yet another day he saw a corpse.

Whatever happiness is in the world has arisen

from a wish for the welfare of others; whatever misery

there is has arisen from indulging selfishness.

—BUDDHIST PROVERB

One act of pure love in saving life is greater than

spending the whole of one's time in religious

offerings to the gods.

—FROM THE BUDDHIST CANON

From that point on, wealth and comfort no longer mattered to him. All his thoughts and energies turned toward solving the world's problems of disease, suffering, and death.

Leaving his comfortable life behind, he sought answers in a life of asceticism, abandoning all earthly pleasures for the simplest of lives. This led only to futility and did nothing to solve the problems of humanity with which he was concerned. But as we will see, his search did not end there.

The Buddhist Pali Canon, considered Scripture by some branches of Buddhism, teaches that prior to his becoming the Buddha, Gautama lived many lives as a *bodhisattva,* someone destined to be a Buddha, but not yet. Those lives were characterized primarily by acts of charity and self-denial. Stories and legends related to the Buddha cite compassion as Gautama's all-consuming motive.

When he sent his disciples out to preach, he told them, "Go ye now, O monks, and wander for the good of many, for the welfare of many, out of compassion for the world, for the advantage, good, and welfare of gods and men."

O that I might become for all beings

the soother of pain.

O that I might be for all of them that ail

the remedy, the physician, the nurse,

until the disappearance of illness.

O that by raining down food and drink I might soothe

the pangs of hunger and thirst, and that in times

of famine I might myself become drink and food.

O that I might be for the poor

an inexhaustible resource.

—SANTIVEDA, SEVENTH-CENTURY INDIAN POET

Gautama became the Buddha following his enlightenment, that is, his full understanding of ultimate reality, of the purpose and destinies of all living beings, and of the guiding principles of the universe. At that point, he could have retired from the world, but instead, out of compassion for the world, he went about sharing his truth, though few would understand. This suggests that followers of Buddhism are not passive recipients of esoteric religious truth, but active participants in the effort to rid the world of ignorance and suffering.

Some have likened the Buddha to a great physician dedicated to curing the disease of *duhkha,* or suffering. This is reflected in the Four Noble Truths that lie at the foundation of Buddhist belief: (1) Suffering exists. (2) There is a cause of suffering. (3) Suffering can be stopped. (4) There is a way, the noble Eightfold Path, to stop suffering.

The Eightfold Path admonishes followers toward right knowledge, right aspiration, right speech, right effort, right mindfulness, and right behavior. It includes an emphasis on benevolence and an aversion to injuring others. Many

Let none deceive another

Nor despise any person whatsoever in any place.

Let him not wish any harm to another

Out of anger or ill will.

Just as a mother would protect her only child

At the risk of her own life,

Even so let him cultivate a boundless heart

Toward all beings.

Let his thoughts of boundless love

Pervade the whole world,

Above, below, and across without any obstruction,

Without any hatred, without any enmity.

—From the Metta-Sutta

Buddhists extend their prohibition on killing to include animals; thus they choose to be vegetarians.

The Buddhist religious tradition focuses heavily on the goal of overcoming ignorance through enlightenment. This task is partly related to knowledge and wisdom, but it also pertains to moral understanding and maturity. Ignorance is defined in terms of self-aggrandizement, the pursuit of selfish desires, and the attachment to the things of the world. Thus, it is the root of evil and misery in the world.

The Buddhist understands enlightenment in terms of karuna, or lovingkindness, out of which comes the commitment to seek the welfare of all humanity. This is the will of the deity, according to Buddhist teaching, and in the deity all human beings are united.

Compassionate, caring, full of love, ready to sacrifice selfish desire for the sake of others—these are the moral qualities of Buddhists who are in touch with their religious heritage. This is agape. And these are the values humanity needs to learn. ❧

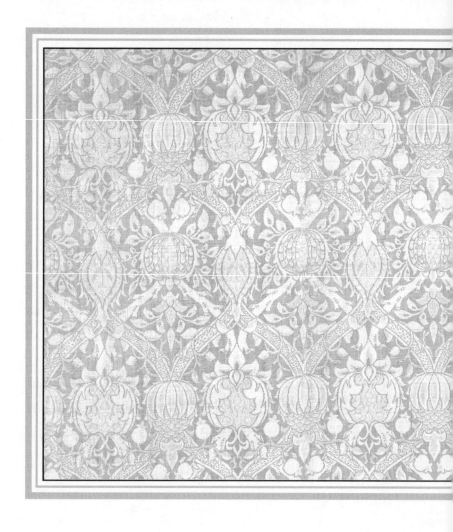

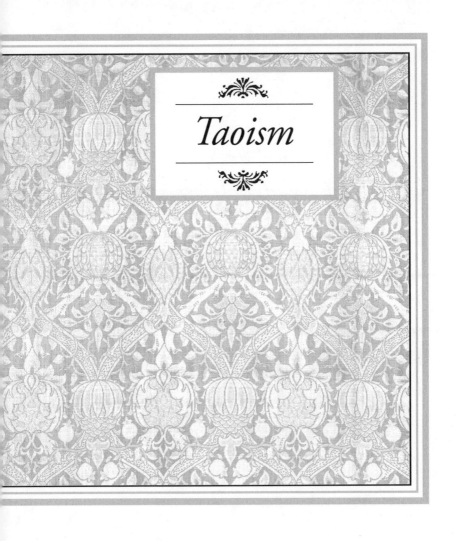

Taoism

The supreme good is like water,

which nourishes all things without trying to.

It is content with the low places

that people disdain.

Thus it is like the Tao.

—TAO TE CHING (8)*

Taoism

Seeing agape in the Tao is like trying to separate a wave from the ocean. It is hard to see either agape or the wave as separate from the whole. The Tao is the spiritual principle that permeates the universe. It is the source, the named and the unnamed, the first cause. To understand the Tao is to understand the light and the life of the universe.

Taoism originated from the writings of a Chinese philosopher named Lao Tzu, who was born approximately 604 B.C.E. These writings were collected in a slim volume called the *Tao Te Ching*, translated as *The Way and the Power*. An older contemporary of Confucius, Lao Tzu advocated a simple, peaceful, unassertive life based on the Tao.

As a religion, Taoism teaches how to live life wisely—by not

Do you have the patience to wait

till your mud settles and the water is clear?

Can you remain unmoving

till the right action arises by itself?

—TAO TE CHING (15)*

He who stands on tiptoe doesn't stand firm.

He who rushes ahead doesn't go far.

He who tries to shine dims his own light.

—TAO TE CHING (24)*

pursuing senseless activity, conflict, and dissipation of energy. This philosophy developed into mastering the use of energy, called ch'i. Martial arts, Chinese medicine, and a unique form of meditation grew out of this way of thinking. By mastering a quiet mind, detached from self-serving motives and senseless activity, the ch'i could flow freely into the practitioner. One who learned to quiet the mind literally could become a catalyst for good and for change by the moral and mystical power that was present.

Today in an age of unprecedented opportunity for peace and prosperity, societies around the world are instead experiencing self-centered stress and social pathology. Something is clearly wrong. The Taoist concept of agape begins with an effort to address what is wrong.

To the Taoist, addressing what is wrong is not so much a question of efficient problem solving as it is a matter of the heart. Despite all our so-called progress, humanity in general is missing something. We are still fighting the universe instead of seeking to understand and work within its ebb and flow. We

Those who embody nobility

to act for the sake of the world

seem to be able to draw the world to them,

while those who embody love

to act for the sake of the world

seem to be worthy of the trust of the world.

—TAO TE CHING (13)†

are out of sync with the Tao, "the way," the meaning of which Huston Smith suggests was well captured by Darwin colleague George Romanes, who spoke of "the integrating principle of the whole—the Spirit, as it were, of the universe—instinct, without contrivance, which follows with purpose."

The world benefits from invention, faster airplanes, more efficient technology. The Taoist is more concerned with inner peace and contentment. The implications for agape are more implied than they are stated. The way of the world is such that many don't care whom they trample upon on their way to fame and fortune. The devout Taoist tramples on no one because fame and fortune are irrelevant pursuits. Material things are superficial; the Taoist quest is a selfless one.

To the Taoist, attitude and behavior are integrated. Proper actions—agape—flow naturally and spontaneously from lives grounded in the Tao, from people who are at peace with the universe and thus with themselves. Taoist values include what Smith describes as an "almost reverential attitude toward humility," an attitude that "led Taoists to honor hunchbacks

Weapons are the tools of violence,

all decent men detest them.

Weapons are the tools of fear;

a decent man will avoid them

except in the direst necessity

and, if compelled, will use them

only with the utmost restraint.

Peace is the highest value. . . .

He enters a battle gravely,

with sorrow and with great compassion,

as if he were attending a funeral.

—TAO TE CHING (31)*

74

and cripples because of the way they typified meekness and self-effacement."

Agape in the Taoist context includes a strong opposition to violence and a high view of the natural world. Smith observes that this stands in stark contrast to the view of nature as "an antagonist, an object to be squared off against, dominated, controlled, conquered." Instead, the Taoist would befriend or attune with the natural world rather than dominate it.

People would do well to understand the relationship between personal peace and social peace, and between self-contentment and loving behavior. One might wonder how many wars were started because of unresolved personal conflicts in the lives of powerful men and women. Taoist values implore us to slow down, reevaluate, reconsider what is truly important and valuable to us, and finally to realign our lives accordingly.

This journey of inner development, a type of yogic process, is intended to remove selfish motives and return to pure thoughts and actions. As the mind goes to its original purity,

True words are not beautiful,

beautiful words are not true.

The good are not argumentative,

the argumentative are not good.

Knowers do not generalize,

generalists do not know.

Sages do not accumulate anything

but give everything to others,

having more the more they give.

The Way of heaven helps and does not harm.

The Way for humans is to act without contention.

—TAO TE CHING (81)*

peace and harmony result. And rather than a passive acceptance of whatever happens, there is a sense of joy, serenity, goodness, and vitality. When one is going with the flow of the universe, rather than resistant to it, true agape may extend to all who come in contact with the person who radiates pure, unlimited love. ❧

*Translations from Stephen Mitchell, *Tao Te Ching* (San Francisco: HarperCollins, 1991). Used with permission.

†Translation from Thomas Cleary, *The Essential Tao* (San Francisco: HarperCollins, 1991). Used with permission.

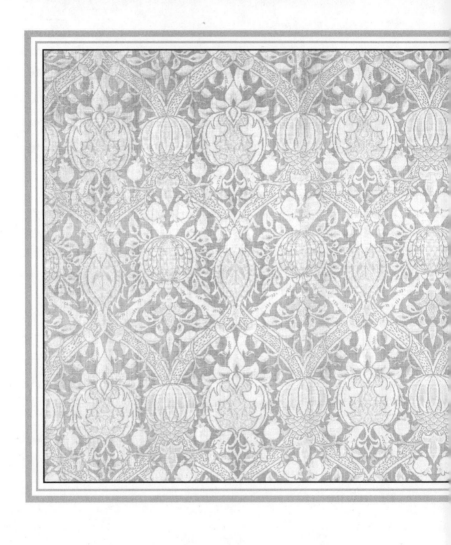

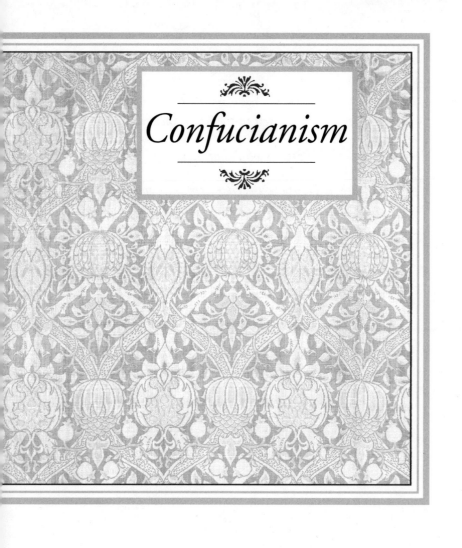

Confucianism

If there is righteousness in the heart, there will be

beauty in the character.

If there is beauty in the character, there will be

harmony in the home.

If there is harmony in the home, there will be

order in the nation.

If there is order in the nation, there will be

peace in the world.

—A PROVERB FROM CONFUCIANISM

Confucianism

The name "Confucius" to many people worldwide is virtually synonymous with "wisdom." His was a wisdom rooted in deep love and respect for others. It is a wisdom that the world always needs.

The philosophies and ideas of Confucius did not emerge from an ivory tower. He was born around 551 B.C.E. into a society that, along with other parts of the world, was experiencing widespread social anarchy. Rival warring factions were invading one another. Prisoners of war were being put to death in mass executions. People were being slaughtered by the tens of thousand. Even women, children, and the aged were routinely beheaded.

These images stand in stark contrast to the meek and gentle

There are four things in the Way of the
profound person, none of which I have been
able to do. To serve my father as I would expect
my son to serve me. To serve my ruler as
I would expect my ministers to serve me.
To serve my elder brother as I would expect
my younger brothers to serve me.
To be the first to treat my friends
as I would expect them to treat me.

—From Confucianism's

Doctrine of the Mean

Chinese culture taught by Confucius. In their introduction to *The Sacred Books of Confucius,* Ch'u Chai and Winberg Chai write of a people who are "profoundly thankful" for three meals a day. And "whatever may be their innermost thoughts, they bear their hardships and privations with admirable heroism."

The ancient philosopher took it upon himself to reinvent the moral and social order of his society. Some social philosophers of his time taught that the only successful way to control human behavior was through brute force. But Confucius built his teachings around the concept of *jen.* Translated as "virtue," "goodness," "charity," or "love," jen is often considered to be Confucianism's expression of agape.

The word jen is formed from the Chinese characters for "humanity" and "two." This reinforces the fundamental ideal of jen, namely, that love finds expression in the context of human relationships. Confucius focused specifically on five relationships: governmental, parental, conjugal, fraternal, and friendship. Many have noted that of the five, three concern the family.

His example first affected his wife,

And then reached to his brothers.

Thereby he governed his home and the state.

—FROM THE SACRED BOOK THE SHIH

This does not mean that the love shared by siblings, or by parent and child, or husband and wife is more important than love for humanity in general. Rather, Confucianism would hold that all forms of love are inseparable, part of the same fabric. In other words, there is a relationship between the way we treat our families and the way we treat our neighbors. There is a relationship between the way mayors and governors carry out their civic responsibilities and the way they treat their spouses and their sons and daughters. It is all a part of the same web of love. It is no small wonder that some of our Founding Fathers, including Benjamin Franklin, were enamored with the political implications of Confucian ideals.

Some people treat love as if it is a quantity that can be exhausted. They are careful not to use it up, not to love others for fear there will be none left for family and friends. But agape is unlimited. It cannot be "used up." In fact, to Confucius it was quite the opposite: the more we love, the more capable we become of loving. ❧

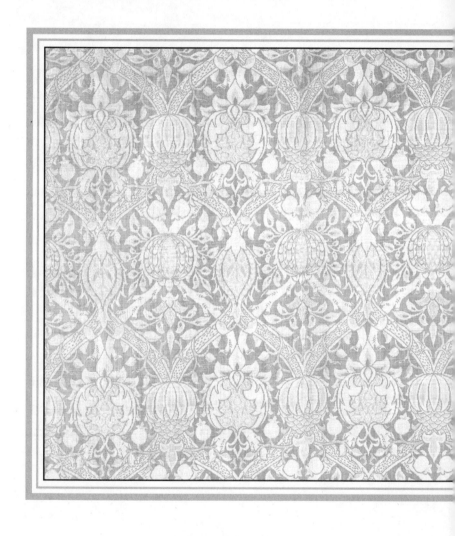

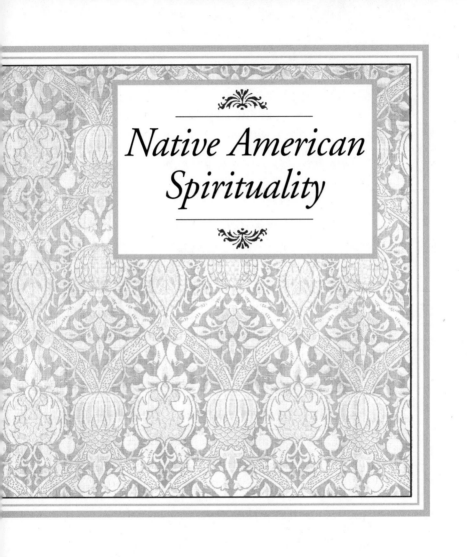

Native American
Spirituality

A peace chief represents peace and compassion.

Our primary purpose is to live a good life,

to set an example for our young people,

our children and grandchildren,

and to teach them about our Creator.

—Chief Rollin Haag

Native American Spirituality

According to my tradition, from the beginning of creation, every morning, when the sun comes up, we are each given four tasks by our Creator for that day. First, I must learn at least one meaningful thing today. Second, I must teach at least one meaningful thing to another person. Third, I must do something for some other person, and it will be best if that person does not even realize that I have done something for them. And, fourth, I must treat all living things with respect. This spreads these things throughout the world.

Spoken by a Cree Native American teacher and storyteller,

Mother Earth is a living spirit that clothes,

feeds, and nourishes all walks of life,

but when fighting erupts, the land

and life cease to flourish,

as well as the spirit of humankind.

—CHIEF ARVOL LOOKING HORSE

OF THE LAKOTA, DAKOTA,

AND NAKOTA NATIONS

it contains a philosophy of life that is at once both simple and profound. Our Creator asks for a mere four actions each day, something eminently "doable." And yet if we were to take these four admonitions seriously, the world might be overtaken by waves of understanding, peace, and agape.

Let us take a closer look at this Cree "prayer." The first goal is to learn something "meaningful" with each new day. The second is to teach something meaningful to another person. "Meaningful" clearly implies something deeper than solving a math equation or sharing with someone a trivial fact that might come in handy.

Goals three and four bring to the daily learning and teaching the dimension of agape. Goal three is to do something for another person to serve that person. But the entry to the door of agape is found in the words "It will be best if that person does not even realize that I have done something for them."

To do something for another with the idea that he or she will do something for you might be described as common-

Whatever befalls the earth

befalls the sons and daughters of the earth.

We did not weave the web of life;

we are merely a strand in it.

Whatever we do to the web,

we do to ourselves.

—CHIEF SEATTLE

sense or practical wisdom. But it is not agape if the ultimate aim is self-serving. To serve anonymously, to love for the sake of loving and not for the hope of reward, is to serve in the spirit of agape.

Jesus talked a lot about hypocrites who performed their acts of charity in broad daylight for all to see. They already have their reward, he said. The Cree prayer, however, speaks of a kind of love that needs no recognition. To serve others is motivation enough.

I am reminded of a story I read once called "Train Man" about a group of children who ran gleefully to the train tracks each Saturday upon hearing the train whistle blowing from a distance. They knew the engineer would be dispensing several handfuls of candy from the driver's side window. The children never knew who this person was. In fact, they could not be sure the Train Man was really a man. But whoever it was did not need or desire any credit or reward. To contemplate bringing a bit of joy to some children's lives was reward enough. The world needs more "train men," more people

One who walks a dark road is distracted,

who is ruled by his senses and who lives for himself,

rather than for his people.

—Black Elk,

Native American spiritual leader

who love with agape, who serve without expecting anything in return.

The fourth aspiration of the Cree prayer is to treat all living things with respect. One of the central characteristics of that Native American religion is its emphasis on caring for all creation—not just other human beings, but birds and other animals and even lakes and fields.

This caring for all of creation, a caring that reflects agape, is rooted in the notion of cosmic harmony, one of the primary characteristics of spirituality. According to some Native American mythology, all creatures were once human until a change took place resulting in the creation of birds and other nonhuman animals. But instead of adopting a sense of superiority over the rest of creation, Native Americans developed an affinity for animals, based on their common heritage. This affinity is reflected in some religious ceremonies where participants imitate animals in dress and in actions.

Agape in the Native American context affirms that everything we see, hear, and touch is part of the web of life. When

You chiefs are peacemakers.

Though your son might be killed in front

of your tepee, you should not take revenge.

Then you would be called an honest chief.

—SWEET MEDICINE,

CHEYENNE TRIBAL HERO

we injure that web, we injure ourselves. When we serve others, we build the web; we strengthen it for the sake of all. To serve with agape is to be willing to learn, to teach, and to give, to love for the sake of love itself, with no expectation of reward. ❧

Concluding Thoughts

In this brief examination of what various religious traditions have taught with regard to agape, many similarities have come to the surface. We see in each tradition admonitions toward peace and love and against violence and hatred.

We see a recognition of the reality that violence inevitably begets more violence. One is reminded of Tevye in the musical "Fiddler on the Roof," who said that if all would live by the saying "an eye for an eye and a tooth for a tooth," the world would soon be blind and toothless. Agape points to a different way—the way of Jesus, Gandhi, Buddha, and many others who were prepared to die, or to allow their selfish desires to die, but were not prepared to abandon agape.

We see a special concern on the part of the world's religions for the weak and defenseless, the vulnerable and voiceless. We see a call to follow in the footsteps of the Muhammad, Confucius, the Old Testament prophets, and many more by seeking to become agents of healing for the suffering of the world.

Although for some, a commitment to agape has entailed martyrdom, to focus on that is to miss the overwhelmingly positive meanings of the word. Agape is active love, love that reaches out to others. It is joyful love, offered not out of obligation, but in a spirit of compassion and hope.

The sentiments of agape are well captured in the classic prayer offered by St. Francis of Assisi:

> Lord, make me an instrument of your peace.
> Where there is hatred, let me sow love;
> Where there is injury, pardon;
> Where there is doubt, faith;
> Where there is despair, hope;
> Where there is darkness, light;
> Where there is sadness, joy.

O Divine Master,
Grant that I may not so much seek
To be consoled, as to console,
To be understood, as to understand,
To be loved, as to love,
For it is in giving that we receive;
It is in pardoning that we are pardoned;
It is in dying that we are born to eternal life.

Unconditional love. Unlimited love. Active love. Joyful love. The option to grow in agape is open to everyone on earth. It is an invitation to true happiness for you and others. May it become our aspiration, our expression of God's love radiating through us. ❧

References and Further Reading

Ali, A. Yusuf. *The Meaning of the Holy Qur'an.* Beltsville, Md.: Amana Publications, 1995.

Bondi, Roberta C. *To Love as God Loves.* Philadelphia: Fortress, 1987.

Bowker, John Westerdale. *World Religions: The Great Faiths Explored and Explained.* London: DK Publishing, 1997.

Carmody, Denise. *Serene Compassion: A Christian Appreciation of Buddhist Holiness.* New York: Oxford University Press, 1996.

Chai, Ch'u and Winberg Chai, eds. *The Sacred Sayings of Confucius.* New Hyde Park, N.Y.: University Books, 1965.

Cleary, Thomas, ed. *The Essential Tao: An Initiation in the Heart of Taoism Through the Authentic Tao Te Ching and the Inner Teachings of Chuang-tzu.* Edison, N.J.: Castle Books, 1998.

Ellwood, Robert S., ed. *Eastern Spirituality in America: Selected Writings.* New York: Paulist Press, 1987.

Herman, A.L. *A Brief Introduction to Hinduism: Religion, Philosophy, and Ways of Liberation.* Boulder: Westview, 1991.

Lester, Robert C. *Buddhism: The Path to Nirvana.* San Francisco: HarperSanFrancisco, 1987.

Mitchell, Stephen. *Tao Te Ching: A New English Version.* New York: HarperCollins, 1991.

Moses, Jeffrey. *Oneness: Great Principles Shared by All Religions.* New York: Fawcett Books, 1992.

Pieris, Aloysius. *Love Meets Wisdom: A Christian Experience of Buddhism.* Maryknoll, N.Y.: Orbis Books, 1988.

Roberts, Elizabeth and Elias Amidon, eds. *Earth Prayers: From Around the World.* HarperSanFrancisco, 1991.

Sherwin, Byron L. *Why Be Good?: Seeking Our Best Selves in a Challenging World.* Emmaus, Pa.: Rodale Press, 1998.

Smith Huston. *The World's Religions.* San Francisco: HarperSanFrancisco, 1991.

About the Author

Born in 1912 in rural Winchester, Tennessee, John Marks Templeton was president of Phi Beta Kappa at Yale University. In 1936 he received a master's degree at Oxford University as a Rhodes scholar, and later twenty-three honorary doctorate degrees. He became a legendary, innovative investment counselor and a pioneer in global investing. Although Sir John retired from business in 1992, the Templeton mutual funds now invest over $100 billion.

In 1972 he founded the Templeton Prize for Progress in Religion, the largest philanthropic monetary award in the world. Now worth more than $1 million, the Prize is given each year to a person whose work has advanced the world's understanding of God in an innovative, creative way. In 1987, the year Her Majesty Queen Elizabeth II knighted him for his philanthropic efforts, Sir John founded the John Templeton Foundation in Radnor, Pennsylvania, whose major donations help fund research in science and religion, spirituality and healing, and character education. The Foundation also supports free competition as a means of helping the poor and teaching ethics.

After launching a new research program in forgiveness in 1997, the Foundation is undertaking a new area of research: agape love. The spiritual principle of unlimited, unconditional love may be a basic reality of the universe, existing before and instrumental in the development of the material world. This book seeks to identify the characteristics, the benefits, and common qualities of agape as it is seen in eight world religions. ❧